D1470438

PRAISE FOR PAT MORA

"Ms. Mora's poems are proudly bilingual, an eloquent answer to purists who refuse to see language as something that lives and changes."

—New York Times Book Review

"Mora celebrates the ordinary in unordinary lyrics."

—Publishers Weekly

"Mora's imagery contributes intensely to her spare and minimalist poems. . . . [Her] poems both instruct and delight."

—Texas Books in Review

"[Pat Mora's] voice is multifaceted: tender, humorous and joyful but also profound."

—Kirkus Reviews

"Mora's radiance and exuberance are simply enchanting."

—North American Review

ENCANTADO

CAMINO DEL SOL

A Latina and Latino Literary Series

ENCANTADO
DESERT MONOLOGUES

PAT MORA

THE UNIVERSITY OF
ARIZONA PRESS

TUCSON

The University of Arizona Press
www.uapress.arizona.edu

ISBN-13: 978-0-8165-3802-7 (cloth)

Cover design by Leigh McDonald

Publication of this book is made possible in part by the proceeds of a permanent
endowment created with the assistance of a Challenge Grant from the National
Endowment for the Humanities, a federal agency.

Library of Congress Cataloging-in-Publication Data
Names: Mora, Pat, author.
Title: Encantado : desert monologues / Pat Mora.
Other titles: Camino del sol.
Description: Tucson : The University of Arizona Press, 2018. | Series: Camino del
    sol : a Latina and Latino literary series
Identifiers: LCCN 2017056368 | ISBN 9780816538027 (cloth : alk. paper)
Subjects: | LCGFT: Poetry.
Classification: LCC PS3563.O73 A6 2018 | DDC 811/.54—dc23 LC record avail-
    able at https://lccn.loc.gov/2017056368

Printed in Canada
♾ This paper meets the requirements of ANSI/NISO Z39.48-1992 (Permanence
of Paper).

For my granddaughter Bonny and my loving family

*But the natural world is the old river
that runs through everything,
and I think poets will forever
fish along its shores.*

— MARY OLIVER

CONTENTS

Acknowledgments	xi
Señor Ortega	3
Encantado	5
José	7
Eduardo	9
Mildred	11
Fumio	13
Phil	15
Barbara	17
Lupe	19
Lydia	21
Rita	23
Tuan	25
Margaret	27
Linda	29
Norma	31
Sister Brigid	33
Father Louis	35
Becky	37
Lucia	39
Anna	41
August Bees	43
Toodles	45
John	47
Rose	49
Branch	51
Amy	53
Dear Amy	55

November 2: El Día de los Muertos	57
Stella	59
Reluctant Death	61
Raúl	63
Monica	65
Twelve Choir Questions	67
Don Arturo	69
Gilberto	71
Rogelio	73
Cecilia	75
Elizabeth	77
Guillermo	79
The River	81
David	83

ACKNOWLEDGMENTS

A special *gracias, gracias* to my family, particularly Vern, Bill, Libby, Cissy, and Stella, who have supported my writing through the years, and my poet friends Father Murray Bodo and John Drury, who read previous drafts of these poems. A special thank-you also to my cheerful friends and helpers: my agent, Elizabeth Harding, and Linda Weston, Bobbie Combs, and the late Laurina Cashin.

I am grateful to the many poets I've read through the years. For this book, I'm indebted to inspiration from *Spoon River Anthology* by Edgar Lee Masters and *Our Town* by Thornton Wilder.

My thanks to the editors of publications in which the following poems or versions of them previously appeared:

"Elizabeth" (originally published as "La osa") and "Sister Brigid." *Pilgrimage* 36, nos. 2/3 (2012): 33–35.

"Lydia" (originally published as "One Potato"). *Spud Songs: An Anthology of Potato Poems*, ed. Gloria Vando and Robert Stewart (Kansas City, Mo.: Helicon Nine Editions, 1999), pp. 47–48.

"Mildred" (originally titled "Uncoiling"). *Daughters of the Fifth Sun: A Collection of Latina Fiction and Poetry*, ed. Bryce Milligan, Mary Guerrero Milligan, and Angela de Hoyos (New York: Riverhead Books, 1995), pp. 40–41.

"Monica" (originally published as "Resistance"). *Feminist Studies: The Chicana Issue* (Spring/Summer 2008): 71.

"Reluctant Death." *The Beacon Best of 1999*, ed. Ntozake Shange (Boston: Beacon Press, 2000), pp. 23–25.

———. *Chelsea 64*, ed. Richard Foerster (Cooper Station, N.Y.: Chelsea Associates, 1998), pp. 188–89.

ENCANTADO

SEÑOR ORTEGA

I live in languages, Spanish, English —
and shoes, yes, old *zapatos*, their leather tongues.
Seventy years of rhythm, my hammer's
tap-tap-tap,
the sewing machine's *whirr*,

quiet *thud*, the screen door —
customers, nodding and shaking my hand,
the old *cortesías* — except for that man
years ago who suggested I change my name
to improve my business. Crazy, some people.

Now, I reluctantly speak the language
of sadness — my wife whose last sigh
got lost inside her worn, weary body
and disappeared into her bones. Alone,
all I hear at home — TV, refrigerator.

Gnarled as tree roots, these hands mend
flamenco taps. My name still on my sign.
I speak words of faith — practice, practice.
I pick up the next shoe or boot — like us,
it needs patient attention and repair.

ENCANTADO

The last nights of the year,
      kind, departed spirits return
to Encantado as stars,
   meander
      down dark streets and hallways,
         peer into windows,
congregate around cribs,
      again leave glowing glints
of themselves;
   intertwine with our dreams,
shine on bare boughs,
      pines, and cactus spines.

JOSÉ

Mamá pulled me, shielded me
>from the body swinging from a limb—
>>*abuelo*, a dark memory.

Was he a *revolucionario*?
>The nightmare.
>>Mamá panting, pulling, pulling me.

I had lived in *español*,
>its comforting syllables.
>>Grudgingly, I learned stiff English.

I learned English and how to sweep my school.
>When the other children ran out laughing—
>>I delivered newspapers, but

a teacher gave me a pencil,
>a tablet. We found quiet corners,
>>we three.

Kind people praised me.
>I became formal in gratitude,
>>At a fancy department store,

I designed scenes for the wealthy.
>Ladies strolled by, polite in their longing.
>>Privately, I longed to sketch.

For years, I painted scenes on city buses.
    Nights, I studied—spurs, saddles.
        With pen and ink, I worked until dawn—

illustrated hundreds of books,
    missionaries I hoped were holy,
        conquistadores, their arrogant horses.

I bowed when the king of Spain knighted me.
    Even the American president bought my work.
        Mexicans—believers, faithful artists.

Old *río*, you and I live in two countries.
    What crooked memories.
        What crooked journeys.

EDUARDO

A desert boy who always loved the West —
slow tales of cowboys round a fire, the stars —
when grown, I drove for years in an old car,
a beat-up wagon minus an AC,
along the border, towns like Eagle Pass,
reviewing ledgers for the government.

Alone, I'd drive along by sage and sand,
the desert and its glare, its grand expanse.
I noticed details to help stay alert,
and that's how I began to wonder, ask,
"Who crossed this place in wagons long ago?

"A hearty people, that much I am sure,
and did their wheels turn here where mine roll too,
and did a boy peek out? Let's call him Juan."
I added details; slowly stories grew,
until I'd ask myself, "So which today?"

When travel stopped, the stories rolled along.
I'd pace the house on winter days and hope
a new idea would soon begin to spin —
a magic blanket for María and child —
un cuento, ah! To entertain my wife.

At ninety, hearing carols, I still see
that lone man on the long road years ago.
I chuckle at my trusty car, odd place,
where stories started offering me new lives,
my private pleasure keeping me alert.

Our days of entertaining now are gone,
the fancy parties my dear wife would plan.
No children came to us, but stories grew —
still entertain this old man in the dark.

MILDRED

With thorns, she scratches
　　on my window, tosses her hair dark with rain,
　　　　snares lightning, cholla, hawks, butterfly
　　　　　　swarms in the tangles.

She sighs clouds,
　　head thrown back, eyes closed, roars
　　　　　　　　　　　　and rivers leap,
boulders retreat like crabs
into themselves.

She spews gusts and thunder,
　　spooks pale women like me,
　　　　who scurry to lock doors, windows
　　　　　　when her tumbleweed skirt starts its spin,

we sing lace lullabies
　　so our children won't hear
　　　　her uncoiling
　　　　　　through her lips, howling
　　　　　　　　leaves off trees, flesh
　　　　　　　　　　off bones, until she whirs,

becomes sound.

FUMIO

How I knew bodies,
their newness, their slow decay.
I knew trust and hope,
eyes entreating me—please, please,
repair what I am.

I knew luxuries
as did my smiling family—
silk's music, art, wine,
strolls in our scented garden,
our koi, captive—were we, free?

Then the rumors, fears.
Our faces in the mirror—
we, Japanese: suspects.
The knock, and I was removed,
yanked from familiar faces.

Wind banged desert shacks.
Strangers, we were bathed in sand.
Erased. We vanished.
I watched my fellow men pace.
Doctors always have patients.

Our eyes, pools of grief.
Cooks, bakers — hands with no work.
One knife, on the counter.
Outside, leaning into the wind,
howling, feeling discarded.

One day, a chuckle.
What a muscle, the human heart.
Our dry, calloused hands
began to carve found wood scraps.
Bent fingers held rough beauty.

An old man, I'm back
to this city and river.
Such tears, nightmares, sighs,
and the wood butterflies. I
watch fragile wings swirl, rise, fly.

PHIL

I remember the jeer —
stung by the kid pointing,
"He can't even tie his shoes."

Their nudges became slugs,
me practicing power
alone — *thud, thud, thud,*
slamming my hate into
the chumps' snubs.
Dad drunk, mom — staring out the window.

I taught myself to prey
on the weak — the fat
boy, the pimpled girl,
the stutterer, the duds
who couldn't even speak English.

Tripping them was fun
trumping their virtue
by a surprise thump
on the ear.

Lucky? Clever.
I excelled: at college
manipulated numbers, profits, egos.

Amazed at the maze the honorable
stumble in, I live concealed
in expensive suits, cars.

I study the big cats.

BARBARA

His insults exploded,
a word storm, lashing
my bones absorbing verbal thrashing,
my skin too thin a shelter,
my voice too thin for me to hear.

His hands never touched me in anger —
only his legal finger — jabbing, jabbing,
jabbing his disgust at me,
my imperfections, incompetence,
inferiority — no spark, a walking failure,
dull — the mother of his three boys.
Listening.

I came to this watery bank, cried with you.
Knelt and washed my hands here
longing to rid myself
of the contamination, me.

LUPE

I'd imagined a different life for myself,

an extension of my young life,
my aunts clapping when I danced,

me spinning, spinning, the dancing
and clapping imagined through the years,

the audience growing,
my daydream smiles too.

Now, I stand behind the counter
when it's quiet between customers,
or chewing my sandwich
under this tree, resting my feet,

I can still return to the spin-
and-smile, my young self unaware—

I'd spend my days in thick-soled shoes,
erased by a uniform,
just grateful to have a job
and a safe place at night.

Sometimes I surprise a customer, ask,
"Did you expect to have this life?"

LYDIA

I buy a potato,
to practice cooking
for one.

Home, I scrub, pierce
the skin, place the sustaining brownness
in the black box, its magic waves.

I set my place
while the potato softens,
then sit, study his chair.

I fold my sadness
in clean creases, over
and over, compressing

until it's the size of a pit
I store inside.
The bell calls me to dinner.

I mash sour
cream, butter, salt, pepper
into the clouds I feed myself.

I taste the altered silence,
bitter and sweet, like plums
that, given time, ripen.

RITA

Winter mornings, Mama—
who was really my grandmother—
placed me in a pool of sunlight
on her well-swept dirt floor.

The wood stove and desert sun warmed
our silence.
You, our river—
the only running water I knew.

Mama sat in a nearby chair, watching me,
gave me space,
maybe teaching me
to live alone.

In the spring, she'd set me
on a patch of grass where I could see
her yellow rosebush.
In the shade, she rocked, accompanied me.

I remember the day she made a gift
for my doll, showed me
how she quickly measured, cut, stitched,
turned the fabric inside out and *poof*!

A dress.

Pleased, we laughed and laughed.
She taught me
my profession.

In her home, my children grown and gone,
she accompanies me again.
In and out of her white lace curtains,
she floats on a breeze.

TUAN

In Saigon, I was an artist, always an artist.
My fingers, even little, liked smoothness—
pencils, pens, brushes—
against my skin, hard, but
a comfort, a hard comfort, strokes
back and forth. I studied
and taught painting in my country.

We had to fly away. Life in California.
I had to learn to paint
nails, careful strokes, to smile
when I washed women's
feet, painted their toes, careful strokes.

I saved, married, and we moved here
to this city with its own river, so much
Spanish. English hard enough.
We worked, saved, bought our nail salon.
Sometimes I painted at home, big paintings.

My English better, nice cars, like technology.
My studio became room for baby.
In our salon, I hang my paintings.
In autumn, I hang trees all gold, a bridge,
peace, all from a postcard, strokes back and forth.
Patrons like my paintings. I smile, but
they don't buy.

I paint nails, pay bills, we survive.
I take my plants out to the edge
of the sidewalk for morning sun.
I help my daughter — her English —
so fine, with her art projects, careful
she paints back and forth.
This week a saint project. What is
a saint? I look on web. I say,
"Dad can help you paint saint."

She likes to paint. I understand.
My wife, delicate but strong, says, "No.
Homework.
Look at us. Doing nails.

Better for her."

MARGARET

I study myself in your ripples,
again choose this river edge,
my wet mirror.

Does my face reveal
the year's losses —
those who slipped away?

Sometimes, I sit on Mother's bed.
Feel relieved, her comfort,
the intimacy with which she looked at me.

Today she surfaces in you —
smiling, arm in arm with me,
as in a dream.

Quickly, I turn my head in expectation,
but I neither feel nor see her —
except here, in you.

I begin to cry, anxious —
I have so much to tell her —
and she may slip away again.

They're all here, friends say —
around us,

but my baby, mom, grandparents —
all bodies
I cherished,
vanished —

a bitter taste — faith.

LINDA

They never change,
the furtive glances at red
panties, black
bras, silk lacy lingerie
I've folded and straightened
for years, buffet for their
imaginations, their whispered,
"Buy something," the woman
or girl, furtive also, slipping into
the store's undressing
rooms. Silence.

Unable to see her own beauty.
Sighs. Whispers—
"So disappointing, my body."

To lift their spirits, when they leave
I say, "Pretty sweater" or "Nice lipstick."
Comfort to strangers, a family—women.

NORMA

I've accepted the habit of falling
in love — gate announcements for music.
I see her ahead of me,
short, her hair, a soft gold,
purse held close,
unrushed — years of experience.
I imagine her hazel eyes, proud
even if she falters.

Greedy, I savor these interludes, solo —
our loves, our creations — solo.
She grins to herself
at some witty, private observation.
Strangers smile back.

For years, airport after airport, a whir
of bodies rushing through
hard surfaces, not a garden —
blooms, breezes, birdsongs,
the setting of my fantasies —
but ever the realist, now a tease,
she appears before me here,
where I can't linger
and strive to lure her to return.

SISTER BRIGID

In the painting, round cows,
black and white,
    and round nuns,
        figures of substance, like me,
move sedately across a field of light,
    nuns erect in their habits,
        gently prodding beasts along,
            like you did, Brigid.

Swollen with energy, you harvested
    corn and gathered lonely women
        all over Ireland
            into rooms safe for song.

Patroness of poets and midwives,
    your wide fingers seduced liquids
        and grains to multiply in your hands,
            butter oozed from your churn,
                dough rose, expanding
across the rough wood table.
    Three times a day, the udders of your cows
        stretched hot with milk.
Clear bathwater foamed gold when you but
    touched it—
        a frothy beer.

Crooning,
    nuns buried you in Downpatrick,
      laid their Mary of the Gael,
        into that dark earth bed.

Round your shrine at Kildare,
    your nuns fed a fire for centuries,
      a round blaze
        no man could pass;
black and white, women of prayer, repair,
    round those flames, dancing.

Here by the river, I rise
    and join their dance.

FATHER LOUIS

Once on a white, rocky path
in Umbria, where Saint Francis sang
a duet with a cicada,
for an instant I heard the earth's
undersong,
the distinct melody of stone,
corn tassel, beetle —
that ripple
around us day after day
like an unheard river.

In my next step,
I returned to the daily whir —
motors, unseen cars, trucks
moving people, goods.

The wise know
that like much that matters —
the undersong
can't be willed,
eludes pursuit.

It can't be earned
by solitude or prayer,
by sitting or walking
attentively —

though such habits could assist
as practice does,

the fingers —
so deep in the piano keys that
they have forgotten the hand —
the body, discovering
a sound that can yield
to devotion.

I try not to try,
though I do preach about miracles.

BECKY

How you splash and spin
after the rains, old *río* —
your noisy celebration
of our celestial blessing
after years of waiting.

For hours, showers rinse trees
dusty with drought, gently
rinse them again.
I watch as their limbs straighten
and lift, a wordless gratitude.

Children's upturned faces, open
mouths, silent choirs lured by
gurgles and puddles,
open lonely umbrellas,
                    splash, stamp
with abandon, free of our fears —
such innocence
                    a second blessing.

I walk my garden paths, remembering
my other *jardines del desierto*,
this demanding land, each bloom
a miniature miracle —
lavish abundance, private surprise —
lavender asters,
                    earthly stars.

LUCIA

Los americanos speak of a bull's power.
At the word, I again feel the hot force
in his belly, see the hooves pawing
years ago, his pupils dilating—

I wish you'd known my Papi.
Éramos del campo. One day—
I am a body of Cuban memories—
an old *toro* blocked our path.

Like high noon in westerns, *el toro* and Papi
stared at one another. My father charged,
grabbed the horns, and held them—eyes bulging,
sweat drenching him—so that Mami and I could run.

That was my father.
No red ruffling cape, no cheering fans,
just a man and a bull
under that blue island sky.

I am a writer. My father can't read or write,
but we are one soul. Brave, he brought us
to the States—the man he was in Cuba—
and not the man he was on his own land.

ANNA

At my desk and in my garage studio,
my doubts occasionally nap.

"*¿Quién será?*
Who can make beauty?"
Mother would challenge.
            At our kitchen table,
               my sisters grabbed Crayolas.
      I'd stare, afraid of ruining
the clean white paper,
        its persistent bareness.

In summer shorts, I sat embarrassed
at my sluggish imagination. I'd watch
flowers and trees bloom
in the gardens
my sisters drew.

At the university, still unable
to join the confidence parade,
I close my office door. Sometimes,
I sketch, but also, I follow my hands—
cut copper sheets, solder,
let the copper lead, with a small torch
anneal brass—heat softens rigidity—
piece together miniature sculptures,

run my hand over the smooth, silky surface,
create Mother's home — kitchen and bedroom —
in a tiny gold birdcage —
confining beauty.
I color the surfaces with pencils,
the wax of honeybees
blends, layers,
retaining its unique colors.

Working expands my soul.

Mother, a widow, a frightened, nervous
woman in her second country,
sits at her kitchen table, begins
her practiced meditation —
her hands rhythmically clean beans,
the familiar easing her into her body.

AUGUST BEES

We feel sluggish, amigo,
woozy with warmth,
the lavish profusion of abundance —
colors, shades, scents, and stems curved, weighted
with blossoms, pollen, nectar —
salvias, marigolds, sunflowers,
honeysuckle — our *bzz-zz-zz*
lulls our very selves to slumber,
our waggle dances, now *zarabandas*,
the bumble, *Bombus sonorus*,
ZZ-ZZ-ZZ, joining your other visitors' murmurs,
whispers, confessions, litanies, fears,
frustrations, doubts, supplications,
romances, extravagant desert sagas.

TOODLES

Carefree me,
a regular at falling
in love speedily.

Time for my eyeballing
in my conservative attire —
my sly play hardly appalling.

Each stroll I desire
relaxing, innocent fun.
Faces to admire.

A quick connection
helps me walk my daily mile.
No introspection

though rhyming a while
also sets a healthy pace,
reminds me to smile.

Three-part merry chase —
walking, wordplay, fantasies.
Hardly a disgrace.

Grinning so slyly,
I eye possibilities —
handsome, eyes friendly —

opportunities,
a possible connection.
My quirky reveries —

first, conversation,
dinners, movies, kissing too,
but wait — hmmm, that one

he's appealing — true,
but I can invest in a new dress —
daydreams, sweet virtue.

Smiles — hard to suppress.
Oops. Late to my rectory desk.
Sassy grin, sinless.

JOHN

A widower, I'm reading
Whispering with Flowers.
Me—an old Romeo.
I long to soften her proper heart.

Unworthy, I must be clever
like my great-grandfather who married
a woman thirty years younger.
I hope Mamande loved him.

I offer Rose the biggest smile
my face can make, but
younger men strut and grin,
flirt and wink.

This is not a winking matter.
I slip secret notes
into books she reads, hoping
she blushes in pleasure.

Her favorite color, purple,
appropriate, meaning dignity—
and, fortunately, also the color of love.
Ah! I'll offer an orchid, symbol of refinement.

My grandson laughs when he sees my book.
I wink. One day, he'll check it out.

ROSE

Eyes closed, I drift
       into my young self,
       the quiet library where Mamá took us.
       Free. The ladies at the desk never spoke
to us but watched, frowned
at our skin and whispers, Spanish.

I imagined myself one day shelving
books, smiling at my patrons.
I read and studied.
I also learned the subtle art
of imitation, to dress and speak properly,
to be like them. Proper?

       One of them, yet never one of them.

I'd rub my hands over worn books
       and smooth, new arrivals. Yesterday,
       wearing purple,
I found an unsigned note
       tucked between pages
       who knows when.
I unfolded the paper.

How I'd longed for such words.

BRANCH

How many nights have I slept
here, wounded, hidden at the edges
of your night sounds, old *río*,
hearing the breeze magnified by trees,
unable to respond
to the calls, "Branch! Branch!"

Am I guilty? Did I kill the man
I startled—the fugitive? madman
who jumped at me
attacking, wrestling me into your waters,
me, gasping to escape; he, pouncing,
pounding, choking me as we thrashed,
gasping, grasping for life—

and when ferociously, like a massive
bear, he flung me
at an old tree bending into your waters,
I hugged a branch and kicked
with all my fury—
and then
                         no resistance,
my heart thumping and yet—
an odd stillness around me.

Did I grab the branch or was I grabbed
by my great-grandfather, for whom I was named—
the obstetrician catching me—
my terrified mind even then
postulating the puzzles of family, irony, language.

Had I killed a man when my boot struck
his chest? Is his breathless body
floating with you
       on your inevitable release to the sea?

I taste dirt, this earth in my mouth.

Why was I saved? Is this what I must carry,
that I clawed my way back into this life
I often feel is a burden
       more than a blessing?

AMY

When I see him stumbling by the river,
I know: Branch has changed.

Is the man whose laugh I love
still dwelling in the exhausted body?

Frightened, we cling together.
He speaks in gasps. "My fury
frightened me,

my life, its earthly salvation: feather-fur-fin,
leaves-limbs, bees-buds-blooms, sun-stars,
rocks-rivers. Dragonflies and hawks living
their lives fret-free, spared overpondered,
endless decisions, the oppressive probability
of error—and regret

and yet, in panic, without free will,
I was unable to resist
the biological imperative: survive."

Another opportunity for despair,
that space he visits too often,
whose dirty, gray windows resist light,
the space I'd entered when he disappeared.

Ever a nurse, I help him shuffle
to a bench by the river, offer
water, yogurt.
He smiles, gulps the comfort.

We listen to the persistent river,
the town's balm.

Self-protective, what time
he has squandered, but

I love the sound of his laugh
that like my father's creates a space,
a place I long to live.

DEAR AMY,

Come and watch me baptize myself
in the river. Symbolic, necessary.
My life: teach, grade, read, listen
to the old *río*, to the stories
it carries, to life's Mr. Ortegas
who says you are a wise nurse,
to the Old Romeo who thumps me
affectionately, loans me
Whispering with Flowers.

I need to find the courage to whisper
and to grapple with fury, less wary.
To stop
dragging you down.

Let's drive away this summer,
see my family and the wide sea.
I long to stare and stare
where rivers release themselves
to new depths, seasoned by the tang
that makes us smart.

Like the river's gold
light and leaves, reflecting
the world's wonder, I need
to float in faith.

I'm writing again, gathering
my young selves.

I wonder: do we ever know
whom we wound?

NOVEMBER 2:
EL DÍA DE LOS MUERTOS

such pleasure—
occasions without the fuss
of details

in we drift
annually gather to savor you
old watery listener

we drift
finally transparent
tiptoe across you and
the streaming stars and moon

rising into a circle   we revolve
gaze down at our humorous
rippling reflections

later drifting again
through familiar dusty streets and rooms
our town

through sounds of the living
patting heads we love
comforting the attentive

                              startling

        our tipsy revelers
disguised as skeletons

        such amateurs

STELLA

I'm fretting again about words,
to your rhythm drifting by.

Will I find the right ones?
Can the doctor, my patient's son, hear
the pauses—implications? Will my words
remove his stethoscope? With a sigh,
will he finally know, feel
his mother is—leaving this earth,
her *is* drifting to *was*—
and all his knowledge, experience,
regular quick visits to check
on her, quick chats
about her diet, fluids, blood pressure—
then rushing back out into his life,
his patients—

will he submit to the inevitable pause?

Can he *see* his mother, her body—
his first home, its weary condition—

a mother and gray-haired son finally
seeing one another—eye-to-eye—
    the conscious stream:

                    acceptance.

RELUCTANT DEATH

I return to your city
reluctantly, this task Brahma
demanded and that I resisted
with supreme asceticism.

For fifty thousand million years,
I stood on one foot.
Brahma said, "Obey my command."
I stood on one foot
for another twenty thousand
million years. I lived with
the teeth and claws of wild
animals for another ten million
million years. "Obey my command."

For twenty thousand years,
I ate only air.
For eight thousand years,
I stood silent in water.
At the Kaushiki River,
I lived only on wind and water,
and at the Ganges and Mount Meru
I stood alone, still
as a piece of wood
to avoid harming anyone.

On the summit of the Himalaya,
I stood on one big toe
for yet another thousand
million years. "Obey
my command," his voice
now feather soft.
"Humans will not blame you."

My teardrops became
the diseases that whisper
to their gauzy flesh, "The time
has come," and I come—
a friend, I hope—
gather them into my palms,
bathe them
with holy water from my eyes.

RAÚL

What did I know? A Mexican kid grateful
for a job, in the rush trying to understand
how to grind lenses for soldiers. In the lab,
trying to read scribbled numbers,
doctors' prescriptions for the perfect 20/20.
Guys shouting about spheres, cylinders, axis,
plus, minus. Greek to me.
Some guy talking about refractions, bending
light, diopters, curves, corneas, retinas.

What did I know? But I learned.
Opened my own lab. United Optical.
Four kids to feed. My hands and eyes, a good team.
Now shouting at my workers, often family,
¡Ándenle! ¡Pronto! ¡Pronto! Rush-rush years,
checking how fast each blank lens
was ground, polished, secured onto its frame
with small pliers, screws — doctors' offices nagging
for faster service, from the man with Mexico always
on his face; gulping lunch, back after dinner.
Payrolls, always the payrolls. The big guys,
national companies, moving in. Had to close.
Sell the house. Move. Kids crying.

What did I know? Such bougainvillea near the ocean.
Me in a nice suit thanks to my wife. Always.

At my desk in a doctor's office fitting frames
on my patients. No rush. Imagine. "Look right at me,"
I'd say and smile, measure with my white PD ruler,
adjust the temples until my patients smiled too.
"Thanks for helping me see," they'd laugh.
Very scientific. A good life, helping people see
better. Never really understood science
like my grandkids. Did what I had to do. When I retired,
my hands grew tired. Nothing to do.

What did I know?
A big man always working and then: nothing.
Bored, I started wandering away from my body.

MONICA

Tía's hands were private,
veined rivers whose blue
mysteries we stroked and stroked,

    in another time, in another place.

Easter streets lined with white
ornamental pears exuberantly wear
the bride gleam she resisted,

    in another time, in another place.

Her laugh drifts through this spring
light, resists the permanence
assigned her dust and bones.

TWELVE CHOIR
QUESTIONS

Is that the cold, old moon humming in the river?
Did the wind's whistle redden the holly berries?
Is it the oven's breath that's sweet with sugar and anise?
Do the pine's daydreams scent the room green?
How do the bells' hearts beat so merrily?
What whispering hands fill our homes with surprises?
Do the *luminarias* guide us to the path of peace?
Who gathers *mano a mano* to shield every child?
Do you hear feathery wings dusting the church with gold?
Are the candles praying together in many tongues?
Can we glow like the shimmers high in the night sky?

We sing, for how can our bodies contain such joy?

DON ARTURO

Soon, I'll amble home,
chat with my love, her photo.
Remember, old *río*, how we would picnic here,
holding hands year after year?

I'll iron my two white shirts,
lulled by the rhythm of erasing wrinkles.
Legs weary, knees aching,
but I must look proper.

My students honor me —
a man who always worked
with his hands. *Imagínate*.
They said, "Be our *maestro*."

After our children married
and she left to wait for me in heaven,
you became my daily consolation,
offering your whispered, liquid secrets
to a man who listens.

"*Por favor*, you know English, don Arturo.
Teach us here, in your home."
They come — grandmothers, uncles,
young mothers — carrying notebooks,
pencils, babies, hope; their bodies
heavy with debts.

I have a desk now, books, paper,
la campanita the students gave me, laughing,
"To keep us in order," and then,
they quietly placed a jar by the door.
They pay what they can.
Weary, they listen as they can.

They look at me, eyes waiting.
O, their spirits shine with courage.
Sometimes, I shuffle papers
to hide my tears.
To share what I know,
well, it's a taste of paradise.

GILBERTO

Grace now, my scruffy canine *compañeros*.
We old dogs must show the way.
We savor mornings and day-old bread
in ways young pups don't understand.

When I was a boy, I'd climb
at dawn to an *arroyo*
that tasted of mint,
water so clear and cold
it hurt my teeth, so sweet
I'd laugh out loud.
I was a mountain lion,
eyes red, body sleek, lean, agile,
poised to pounce,
gnaw impatiently on life.

Now my ankles and knees
teach me to taste my days,
slowly. I make pronouncements
only you heed, but
I still burn, shake my fists,
consoled by my own voice.

ROGELIO

When Rosa and I walked through the dark,
sagging house we could afford—
even with the cobwebs—we felt its promise,
para la familia.
In and out we walked, in and out, in
and out, pacing the first land
we would own here. Ours.
Adiós to the trailer years, the *ps-ps* gossip,
the flirting widow.
In the kitchen with the broken window,
we laughed out loud—us, royalty.

At night, after a long day of planting trees
for a rich man, I began sketching
and grinned as I imagined
glass floors for our humble *adobe* palace,
glass floors with a river—you—flowing, visible
under our feet in every room.
"*Ay, Rogelio,*" sighed Rosa.

Reality is too present—wood, nails, tile—
repairs necessary, but a man needs to imagine
a *río*'s hum under every room
of his first American home.

CECILIA

Slowly, I learned the pleasure
of resting my hands on the hidden
growing that began to precede me.
My slender self, expanded.
I became capacious.

My tenant and I strolled by you —
water within — and you,
rippling by carrying sunlight.

Even while I slept, the divisions
continued, my wee moon grew.
Predictably, she escaped
                        with a gasp.

The first time she smiled at me,
I stopped breathing.
I had to remind myself
to inhale.

Wordlessly, casually, she graced me,
the girl who'd floated inside me —
baptized me with her approval.

The smiles became her melody.

ELIZABETH

If I woke as a bear, my skin covered by shaggy black
fur, I'd eat apples on my haunches, lumber along, stare
at one butterfly all morning in a crimson apple-daze,
unaware of minutes or hours. I'd follow the sun,
dimly smell the pine perfume my paws had climbed,
feel green through and through, in my meanderings
hope to spy my trio, imagine them rambling, their
scents rolling in the grass while I stood so tall I'd pat
the tops of trees. Splashing and smacking the river,
I'd fish with patience, foreign as loping on all fours.
My heart would expand. Winter, I'd dream to the rhythm
of a sarabande, *tramp* *tramp* *tramp*.

GUILLERMO

q u i e t e r
than a puppy crying
all night even when I cover
its face with my blanket

q u i e t e r
than a kitten whining
all night even when I push
its mouth in a bowl of milk

q u i e t e r
than a mouse scritching
all night even when I put
it on a bed of fresh leaves

my turtle will tuck itself in
at night, I tell Mama, and I will dream
of riding down the river
                    on its huge back to the sea.

THE RIVER

In the light is a land.
In the land is a river.
In the river is a song.
In a city flows the song.

To the river come the voices.
Stories in the voices.
Sorrows in the stories.
Longings in the sorrows.
Prayers in the longings.
Hope in the prayers.

Prayers in the hope.
Longings in the prayers.
Sorrows in the longings.
Stories in the sorrows.
Song in the stories.

Song in the river.
River in the land.
Land in the light.

DAVID

My fingers touched smooth piano keys.
I listened to their rambling song.
As my hands grew, they learned to please
as we explored more complex keys —
heard *arroyos*, the teasing breeze,
followed their music, weaving a song.
My fingers touched smooth piano keys.
I listened to my rambling song.

I seek surprises in intimate keys,
compose my elusive life song,
explore repetitions, curious — tease
variations in cascading keys.
I tend harmonics in the breeze,
hear the *río* streaming its song.
I seek surprises in intimate keys,
compose my elusive *canción*.

ABOUT THE AUTHOR

PAT MORA is an author, speaker, educator, and literacy advocate. She has written more than forty-five books for adults, teens, and children. Her poetry collections include *Chants*, *Borders*, *Communion*, *Agua Santa: Holy Water*, *Aunt Carmen's Book of Practical Saints*, and *Adobe Odes*; her books of nonfiction include *Nepantla: Essays from the Land in the Middle* and the family memoir *House of Houses*. The recipient of two honorary doctorates and a poetry fellowship from the National Endowment for the Arts, she lives in Santa Fe, New Mexico.